The A
Accompanying

Phil Daughtry

Maxine Green

immortalise

First published in 2020 by Immortalise
Text © Phil Daughtry, Maxine Green 2019
Illustrations © Mandy Anita Powell

National Library of Australia Cataloguing-in-Publication entry:

Author/s:	Daughtry, Phil. Green, Maxine.
Title:	The Art of Accompanying
Edition:	1st ed.
ISBN:	978-0-6486957-8-3 (pbk)
	978-0-6486957-9-0 (ebook)
Subjects:	1. Accompanying, 2.Care of the soul,

3.Spiritual formation, 4. Helping conversation

Printed Worldwide by: Ingram Spark, via Lightning Source
Internal and external typeset layout by: Ben Morton
Cover photography and image design: Zelma Green
Illustrations by: Mandy Anita Powell
Editing by: Saskia Capon

The Art of Accompanying

Disclaimer

The material in this publication is of the nature of general comment only, and does not represent professional advice. It is not intended to provide specific guidance for particular circumstances and it should not be relied on as the basis for any decision to take action or not take action on any matter which it covers. Readers should obtain professional advice where appropriate, before making any such decision. To the maximum extent permitted by law, the author and publisher disclaim all responsibility and liability to any person, arising directly or indirectly from any person taking or not taking action based on the information in this publication.

God let us be serious.
Face to face.
Heart to heart.
Let us be fully present.
Strongly present.
Deeply serious.
The closest we may come
to innocence.

Amen

(Michael Leunig)

CONTENTS

HOW TO READ THIS BOOK

The keys to reading this book for maximum benefit are curiosity, contemplation and observation. We have not attempted to write a comprehensive and systematic volume. Rather, we are offering a selection of narrative and philosophical views on the topic of accompanying. Our goal is to spark points of connection and resonance and to evoke curiosity and movement. If you expect to receive a watertight and complete explanation of the theory and practice of accompanying, then it would be helpful to recognise that this expectation cannot be fully met as it is outside of the scope and intention of this text.

That's okay. Allow yourself to feel the momentary disappointment and then, when ready, open your hands, gently allow that expectation to float away downstream. Notice in its place a feeling of peace and quiet joy. A sense of walking into a beautiful space without the need to capture, document, codify of otherwise possess it. Just to be in it, receive from it.

What sparks your curiosity and imagination as you read? What sections of the text invite you to pause, slow down, and dwell with a story, idea, point of connection? What do you notice within yourself in the process of this contemplative approach? Does an image slowly emerge and become visible? Is there a flash of insight from a deeper or more transcendent space? Is there a feeling or bodily sensation that it is good for you to feel at this time? Can you allow these encounters and insights to happen and to be themselves without needing to label or categorise them into a systemic form? What kind of gentle response is your life calling you to in relation to your reading experience?

In short, the best way to read this book is to pay close attention both to the text and to the conversation between the text and the fullness of who you are as a reader, body, emotions, intellect, and spirit. Read slowly.

Read the part or parts that call to you today, in this moment. Resist the temptation to master the text or its subject, choosing instead the kinder way: enjoyment, wonder, questioning for its own pleasure and for the space that it opens within you and before you rather than for 'answers'.

There are two voices that speak to the topic of accompanying in these pages. Maxine's voice is more narrative and conversational. Phil's voice leans in the direction of the philosophical and conceptual. There are points of connection and correlation between the voices and there are points of divergent expression. The divergence is not contradictory to the correlation as both voices play within the larger space of the generous idea which we name as accompanying. Our voices are not caged by narrow lines of rigid definition. Accompanying is a free-range activity where there is room to move and breathe and explore the multitude of ways that one may support the expression of the inner life.

There is no wrong way for you to read this book. The way that you read this book is the right way for you to read this book. Its life is larger than the sum of its authorship and readership. Enough said, go outside and play.

FOREWORD

Accompanying is like a golden nugget – a concept which encompasses a special and deep encounter where exchanges are meaningful and life-changing.

I first came across this concept when writing a book for the Church of England with my friend and colleague Chandu Christian. We had been asked to write a book about relationships between youth workers and young people, and when the idea of accompanying emerged it seemed to encompass the very beautiful times when both the young person and the youth worker recognised the gift that comes from an accompanying relationship. The book, *Accompanying Young People on their Spiritual Quest* was very warmly received, and three editions were published before it moved to be published on demand, and it is still selling.

We wrote that book nearly twenty years ago, and since that time accompanying has been adopted as a way of working with young people by Christian youth workers. We recognised early on that accompanying was not just for young people and that there were those in the church practising this across the ages. We also have come to see that this is not isolated to Christians, but that there are people of other faiths and no faiths who are able to achieve this deeper connection and offer a more profound experience through their relationships with others.

By 1999 the book had been 'discovered' by colleagues in Australia, and I was invited to speak at a Diocesan conference in Newcastle, Australia where there was a similar recognition of accompanying and a real joy at finding a word to explain this practice. One woman came up to me after a talk and said that she had been searching for her vocation; she had tried preaching, 'hospitality' in the church, and flower arranging without brilliant success, and then she said, 'I know what I am now – I accompany people.'

Over the years since the first book many people have practised accompanying and we have come to realise how powerful this deep listening is. At the same time many other strands of work have entwined and enriched the accompanying journey. One very fortunate strand occurred when Phil Daughtry from Tabor College Adelaide came to undertake a fellowship at Durham University. As part of his fellowship he was able to share some of his thinking and scholarship and help a small group of us meeting in Durham to explore the role of the spiritual in youth work practice. This was the start of a productive and interesting journey between the UK and Australia, the first of which events was an inspired and inspiring conference in Adelaide, Australia in 2014 called 'Burning Conversations', where practitioners were invited to reflect and share on how spirituality was part of their work with young people. A book was produced from the conference called *Spirituality for Youth-Work: New Vocabulary, Concepts and Practices* (Daughtry & Devenish, 2016.) which has been a real contribution to the field.

Phil was made a fellow of the YMCA George Williams College where I was Principal and helped the college to reflect on the future in a more spiritually informed way that was deeper than the usual business advice from a colleague.

Following this Phil invited me to Tabor College in Adelaide as a 'Thinker in Residence' where I offered to accompany staff and students there during my seven-week stay.

Phil and I took this opportunity to deeply reflect on what accompanying is and how the practice can be shared and developed. Something very interesting emerged from these reflections; we began to see that though the practice of accompanying is important, what is more important is the spirit and experience of the accompanist. We recognised that in the first book the deeper nature of the accompanist was implicit, and the main focus was on the 'how to' of accompanying. We also recognised that the soul of the accompanist was at the heart of the practice and that it would be good to explore this in a more explicit way. We also wanted to embrace the practice and stories of others as they had used accompanying in their lives and work. You will notice that Phil and I have alternated chapters; whilst we share the sentiments of each other's work, we wanted to give freedom to our individual voices and hope that by doing this we will enable readers to tune into different ways of looking at accompanying. We hope that the book will offer a series of lenses to view accompanying through and that the reader will find different elements of the book resonating with their own soul.

This has been quite a journey and one which has been launched from and informed by the wisdom and learning of Chandu Christian who found the first nugget of the idea. We hope that this book will help to bring some more learning and clarity but mostly will be a chance to celebrate the wonderful gift of accompanying.

THE STORY BEGINS

There are moments in life which are special - golden moments, moments like diamonds when there is inner connection and deep beauty. Some of these are conventional moments where one is expected to feel joy, sorrow or be uplifted - the birth of a baby, the beautiful view on the horizon, the crescendo of a magnificent piece of music. Some moments slip in - almost under the radar and surprise us. At these moments it is not only the heart that rises, it is the soul that flies. The soul is nourished and its presence is deeply acknowledged.

11

This is the spirit of accompanying – a beautiful gift to another person, a chance for their soul to be acknowledged, to be able to shine and that deep soul voice to be heard.

Accompanying as a practice has been going on in all sorts of places over many, many years. It is found in different traditions and cultures. It is a beautiful, beautiful practice that has nourished souls in many places and in many ways.

However, accompanying is often accidental as two or more people find themselves in a deeper conversation. The aim of this book, and for the company of accompanists, is to share and develop ideas about what works well and the essential truths of the practice so it can become more available and more helpful.

We recognise that this 'soul work' is not easy to write about so we are happy and confident about using stories and metaphors. We invite you to bring your own story to the text so it makes sense for you.

Dan's Story - Performance and accompaniment

In high school, I learnt to play the Double Bass. My music teacher would encourage her students to participate in an annual local eisteddfod. She would accompany her students on piano for their performance. To teach me the instrument and then to accompany me on the piano required that she be highly skilled in both my instrument and at the piano (she was also skilled at a reasonable number of other instruments). More than just a backing track, as an accompanist she would support and enhance her students' performances. If I was weak in a section of the song, she might play slightly louder to distract from my mistakes. If the mistakes were larger, she might adapt the song during the performance by playing faster/slower or skipping sections. At the end of the performance, I would be judged and did occasionally receive an award. Looking back, I have realised the gift of her accompaniment. She didn't receive an award, despite being more skilled than me and making me sound better. I was the one to gain any recognition of success. Yet success was in large part a result of the care, support, careful listening and adaptation on the part of my teacher.

We all have a story; we all have different traditions. Most of these are helpful and guide and support us as we grow and live. Sometimes though these stories keep us on the surface of our lives, skating on the ice oblivious to the movement of the water beneath us. While we have accompanied others, we have had the joy of listening to other stories, stories that are deeper and engage with our souls. We have also watched as those we have accompanied have heard the deeper story in their own experience. They have known the occasion or encounter was special, but they suddenly discover the hidden depths that have carried meaning and beauty for them.

Dan's story - Silence and Surfing

A significant part of my daily routine in my teenage years was the 'dawn patrol' with my dad. The dawn patrol is the practice of going surfing at daybreak. Two or three times a week we would get up before sunrise, pack boards and wetsuits into the car and drive to the local break. If the conditions were right, we would paddle out into the surf, often in the half-dark, and surf for an hour or two before heading off to school and work. Despite the crashing waves there is calm and meditative space in the soft light of the morning and cool touch of the elements (air, water, sand). Sometimes one of my brothers would come or there would be other strangers and friends who would join us. We would sit on our boards sometimes a metre apart, at other times it could be 20 metres apart, just waiting for the waves. Sometimes there was a lot to talk about, and other times there was just silence. There is always a small amount of danger in surfing, so we were always attentive to the whereabouts of the other person. We look out for each other. In silence or conversation there is a presence, a sense of care and being known. Upon reflection, this time spent with my dad in such a simple and mindful space was surely a firm foundation for my developing sense of self and experience of the world.

Accompanying has its roots in the Latin word for bread which is *panem* and *com* which means with. Accompanying means 'with bread'; it is the relish that gives spice, colour and interest to life. This is an exciting offer, and a notion in the world that is continually undervalued as we look at dully efficient ways to complete tasks or duties. What a great world it would be if we encountered those who had this extra relish and joy as they went about their daily work.

In one accompanying experience a young woman recognised that some of the love she was trying to give to all of those around her should also be for her. That her own soul needed love, care and attention and to be valued as the beautiful thing it was. For her this started a journey of freedom and peace. Not surprisingly it not only helped her, it fed and nourished the souls around her.

Sometimes life is particularly hard and the soul suffers and feels eroded or crushed. At times like these we are tender and extraordinarily sensitive. If we can find a soul to accompany us and help us to open these wounds and sores to the light and love it can be a source of great healing and beauty.

This is a time when the sensitivity of the accompanist comes into play. When we encounter sadness and pain it is really difficult to walk with the person while seemingly 'doing nothing'. The temptation to fix the situation, locate good ideas and to make it better can be immense. The accompanist knows that this, however tempting, is not the most helpful way to support. It detracts from the central position of a deep belief that the heart and the mind of the person accompanied has an answer that most deeply resonates and is right for their own soul.

When I wrote *Accompanying Young People on their Spiritual Quest* with Chandu, it helped me remember my teacher Miss Golding who, when I was just 7 years old, accompanied me. As a difficult and not-fitting-in sort of child, most teachers squashed me and made me conform – not Miss Golding; she believed in me and had one of my poems published. I located Miss Golding after the book was published and thanked her – tears streaming down my face when I was able to recognise her care and love for me.

I sent Miss Golding a copy of the book, and it arrived on her doormat as she was leaving the house to see a close friend of hers who had just been diagnosed with cancer. She came back home upset, lost and didn't know what to do. At that point she picked up the book, started reading and says she 'suddenly realised what I had to do; I could accompany my friend through her journey with cancer'.

Accompanying like this requires a strong core, a deep connection to the inner centre of peace of the accompanist. Holding this calm centred space whilst

17

another person is in the middle of chaotic emotions brings a comfort and certainty that, in the words of Julian of Norwich, 'all will be well and all manner of things will be well'. It adds that quiet hope and assurance that puts the turmoil on a much bigger stage of eternity. This enables the massive problems of an accompanied person not to be overwhelming or impenetrable but to be placed in an eternal setting of calm and rightness. An accompanist holds that hope with gentle joy and certainty.

When Chandu and I first 'discovered' accompanying our first reflection was on what the accompanist did. These skills are undoubtedly there in accompanying: deep and careful listening, awareness of the ego, and holding the space; however, as we have both used the model and seen others using it, we realise that the key element of accompanying rests elsewhere. It is not so much what we do as accompanists but who we are.

The most significant part of the accompanist's gift is the journey, the self-awareness and the attention that the accompanist has given to their own soul. Paraphrasing St Augustine: 'love God and do as you want'. St Augustine held that a soul who loves God will naturally conform and do the acts that please and honour him. Similarly, the accompanist who has attained a degree of self-awareness and facility to access their soul and beyond will bring this as their primary gift to the encounter. Everything they do will be grounded in this, and everything they do or are will be drawn from their own soul experience.

This quiet 'tuning in' experience can be helpful for the personal practice of the accompanist as they learn about themselves in relation to nature, the world and their God. I believe it also can happen while accompanying others. The accompanist can practice still awareness whilst walking alongside another, and by inhabiting the inner self they can invite the accompanied person's inner self to be more visible and more present.

In a world where many of us are frenetically busy and strained, there is an acute need for soul wisdom - those who have the ability and the inclination to access deep peace, and offer this to other souls. Often these wise people do so in isolation possibly underestimating their own potential contribution – instead thinking that they are just offering human comfort and kindness. It is a dangerous thing to announce oneself as wise, so the gift often lies latent or is available to just a few.

Through this book we want to celebrate 'The Art of Accompanying' so that we can enable the art to flourish and spread. We want those who see this role emerging in their practice and in their lives to grow as accompanists. To courageously walk their inner journey, developing skills but more importantly the capacity and wisdom of their souls.

A company of accompanists sounds lovely too, a group of good folk who can bring this dimension of soul being to those they encounter who can enjoy and learn from each other to build the 'Art of Accompanying'.

Painters on the Left Bank in Paris in the early 1900s inspired each other to become creative, full of passion and commitment to the idea of impressionism. In the same way, bringing human gathering and inspiration to the accompanying endeavour should bring lovely results.

Thank you for joining us by reading this book, we look forward to the gathering of accompanists growing and thriving.

Phil's comment:

I was struck by one of Maxine's early statements in this chapter: 'conventional moments where one is expected to feel ...'. Perhaps accompanying is the gift that allows us to feel what we actually feel in relation to conventional moments rather than what we are expected to feel. This involves us in a journey towards truth. A truth deeply grounded in the reality of our individual unique construction and the ways in which we experience and interact with our very particular situations and circumstances.

Maxine also speaks of the moments that 'slip in – almost under the radar and surprise us'. Her crafted stories illustrate the ways in which an accompanist helps us to recognise these moments and their significance.

I take away from this chapter the importance of assisting people to bear respectful, honest witness to the truth of their own lives and their unique experience of special moments, both conventional and unscripted.

In the following chapter I speak of the qualities that enable such an approach and presence.

QUALITIES OF THE ACCOMPANIST

Accompanying is a practice of being with another in a certain way. This way of being offers an invitation for the person being accompanied to enter a deeper space within themselves. This space within is the sacred heart of the person, a place of peace, of providence, an existential awareness of okay-ness, of being loved, of having a home in a benevolent universe. Thus the primary quality of the accompanist is that he or she will be regular travellers to this space within themselves.

An accompanist is one who has found a path to their own inner space. This means that they have done the work of exploring, evaluating and naming a range of spiritual practices that enable them to centre and re-centre their lives on a consistent basis. It means that they have found the courage to face and come to terms with the shadow sides of their lives in honesty, humility and confession. It means that they have discovered within themselves an original grace, from which flows a stream of compassion and mercy. It means that they have learned to embrace and care for the whole of the actual person they really are with humour, joy, and appreciation. It means that they have touched a mystery larger than themselves and the material world and have been enchanted by its wonder and bigness. It means that they have dug a well into kindness, gentleness and peace. From this safe and grounded space, the accompanist offers a personal presence that non-verbally invites the accompanied to travel their own path to similar wells.

> when I knock on the door of their interior life
> and they let me in, they usually lead me only
> into ... the dingy rooms of their ordinary
> surface life [rather than] ... into the inmost
> chamber of their hearts where the eternal

> spark in them is sick unto death ... on which
> the candles of faith, hope and love should be
> burning ... And thus it is that one who is
> entrusted with the help and care of souls can
> draw near to them only by drawing near to
> You, O King of all hearts. (1999)

In this quote the theologian and priest, Karl Rahner (1904-1984), reflects on the irony of training for a vocation of soul care only to find that no one wants to engage him in conversations of deeper meaning! Yet he concludes that God is present at the centre of all people and that, therefore, as he deepens the space within himself, the silent witness of his own spiritual presence will awaken and call to the latent depths of the other.

The accompanist is one who has cultivated the discipline of presence and attentiveness to the other. They have recognised, named and silenced the voice of their own ego-centrism in the helping relationship. From the ground of their own centred being, they no longer need to be the star of a therapeutic or educational show. They have made friends with the limitations of their intellect, knowledge and skill and have let go of the need for a seamless delivery of service. The accompanist will simply bring the small loaves and fishes of who they actually are, in a radical humility and generosity.

The gift of accompanying is not style, it is substance, the bread of life, whole hearted presence and attention. The nutrients of such bread are not therapeutic techniques but the qualities of a deeper life. The accompanist exhibits a peace that allows the accompanied, for a moment at least, to enter the slipstream of a way of being that is present, calm and still. The accompanist exhibits a kind honesty about themselves which allows the accompanied also to touch base with the various truths of their own stories without shame or disclaimer. The accompanist brings a clarity of seeing through the act of attentiveness. What has been blurred by the fragmentation of ceaseless worry, unnamed fears and frenetic distraction, now comes into focus in the concentrated gaze of calm hospitality. The small signs of hope, goodness and accomplishment in the story of the accompanied are magnified at the same time.

> God help us to find our confession;
> The truth within us which is hidden from our mind;

The beauty or the ugliness we see elsewhere
But never in ourselves (Leunig, 2014)

The accompanist is listening for the silences between the sounds in the narrative of the accompanied. This is a discernment of resonance, a sensing of the deeper pulse of the true life of the accompanied. A person may speak of the many things that preoccupy their consciousness but the accompanist is listening for faint strains of the unconscious melodies that form their original song. Social taboos, critical inner and external voices, the press of circumstances and competing demands may have all but silenced a person's capacity to name and embrace their deeper impulses and genuine desires. Yet such impulses and desires are there and may be recognised by their capacity to evoke joy, freedom, congruence and happiness. The accompanist has an acute radar for that fleeting, half-moment of honesty and connection. That flash of joy and spark of life that is quickly re-suppressed with deference to a familiar, socially compliant script. Over the space of a conversation or series of conversations, the accompanist begins to see a converging pattern in the kaleidoscope of these colourful sparks. At just the right time in the conversational process, the contour and colours of a person's true life are named and offered for consideration. A mirror of the person's actual inner beauty is held up to them. The reflection is shocking and confronting as it defies convention, yet it is deeply attractive and once seen cannot be unseen. Such a process allows the deep to appeal to deep.

Sandra tells her accompanist about a guilty secret. Last Sunday she woke up with the feeling that she just couldn't face another morning at church. She felt instead, a strong desire for a long morning walk in a nearby forest, followed by a quiet coffee and a time of writing in her journal. She couldn't quite bring herself to tell her husband, Ben, an active and enthusiastic leader in the congregation. So she lied, saying she was feeling unwell and thought it would be the responsible thing to rest in an attempt to prevent sickness and lost time at work. She felt terrible for a while but went for the walk anyway and experienced the forest drawing her out of the moral dilemma and into a place of connection and centredness. As she recounts this her face lights up and there is a different energy about her. Then the energy fades as she talks about confessing her lie to God (she can't yet cope with telling Ben) and telling herself that she will make a commitment to attend regularly from now on. Her accompanist hears the resonance of a longing for rest, contemplation and connection to land. He also feels with Sandra her entrapment and confusion in the return to conventional ritual.

The capacity to listen to a story in this way is one that is cultivated and draws on a range of inner and intellectual qualities. The accompanist requires an understanding of soul and spirit that includes sensitivity to faith and philosophical traditions and yet is not bound by them. A deeper awareness of the common aspects of spirituality as a human phenomenon, and also a central process for the discernment of authentic and inauthentic spirit, is required. The courage to engage with the accompanied in the actual truth of the deep soul resonance that reveals itself in freedom, joy, peace and compassion is essential. The accompanist will have made their own journey in such discernment and have taken their own risky steps in treading the authentic path. Such deep listening is not for the fainthearted or for those who cannot bear with misunderstanding or controversy. The accompanist is one who is grounded deeply in the organic soil of their own true life and who is able, from this position, to assist others in hearing and responding to the voice of their own inner depths.

The final qualities in relation to accompanying that are important to mention are 'clunkiness' and vulnerability. An accompanist is required to act with courage but will also inevitably feel fear. At times, the accompanist may recognise that the voice of fear has held them back from the expression of a deeper instinct. Being honest and generous with oneself about this is far more important and necessary than always getting it 'right'. At times, the accompanist will miss the timing of an observation, question or story. At times, the words they use will not seem polished or as exact in meaning as might be desired. The willingness of the accompanist to offer themselves as they are, with the best of intentions and varying levels of finesse, is part of the gift and the point. We have far too many voices of false perfection with which to contend as it is. Therefore, accompanying will not let the perfect become the enemy of the good. Rather, in humility, grace and humour, the accompanist is willing to feel the fear and to bear with the clunkiness of their own capacities in an offer of authentic spiritual companionship. The focus of accompanying quite simply is service rather than accomplishment.

Maxine's comment:

In this chapter I am reminded by Phil of the courage one needs to accompany or to be truly accompanied. In a world where there are social constraints and taboos, it takes bravery and courage to be real to oneself and to be real with others. Walking with others in a deep way requires an internal patience to learn and gentleness with ourselves as we deepen conversations and encounters, and as we deepen our listening so that we feel those hidden depths.

In the next chapter I explore how to reach the deeper inner space and how that relates to us as accompanists.

THE ART AND PRACTICE OF ACCOMPANYING

We have looked at the qualities and fruits of accompanying in the previous chapters; now we turn our attention to what is happening when two people meet for an accompanying session.

Our experience is that this is a joint walk of faith, a conversation of two souls, a trusting time where both parties proceed with a different sort of approach into the sacred space held by the accompanist.

Inevitably trying to write this down is an imperfect process where the words deputise inadequately for the feeling. However, this imperfect process we hope will enable some insights and connections in you, the reader, that you can use as you grow in the art of accompanying.

Being prepared – long term and immediately before the session

The principle gift of the accompanist lies not so much in what they do but in who they are. Occupying and inhabiting the deeper reaches of the soul is only possible where people have done their own 'spiritual work' and wrestled with themselves and their God whatever that means to them. This enables the accompanist to feel at home in the deeper inner space. It will be somewhere that they visit often that informs their everyday life.

Just before the accompanying session the accompanist needs to prepare themselves. The heart of the accompanying process is the deep level at which the conversation occurs. Immediately before a session begins the accompanist needs to go into that space. Learning to dip into the soul, to the quiet essential place of life, is a beautiful skill. As an athlete exercises precise muscles so

34

that they can perform well, the accompanist exercises the ability to locate their own soul space and be able to go into it at will. Prior to the session the accompanist will be in that place of silence and hold an awareness of the importance of this space in the session ahead. This is not necessarily a long process but is nevertheless an essential one. In different ways the accompanist will pause from their busy life and become mindful of the presence of their own soul and the more important and profound elements of the universe, and create a sacred space ready for the accompanied person to enter.

A metaphor that has worked well with me is to imagine a deep pool or ocean. On the surface of the ocean are things that float: flotsam and jetsam. These are buffeted around by the wind and are subject to turbulence and disturbance. This top level represents the activities we are involved in and the drama of our lives.

Going deeper into the ocean there is not so much turbulence – this is the area where our feelings operate. Feeling safe and secure can give a base to the activities above but can also create strong undercurrents that affect and disturb our lives and what we do.

Going deeper still we are further from the surface and are not so affected by the drama of our everyday lives. This is an area of logic and analysis, where we use our minds and reason to explain, predict and motivate ourselves.

Deeper still at the depths of the ocean represents our spirit. If we bring our consciousness and attention to this level, there is a peace. There could be a hurricane above the sea which can dramatically disturb us, but if we can deepen our consciousness to the levels of the spirit, although we will still experience these dramatic activities, our soul will be in a safe calm space, able to make decisions and actions with the security and deep knowledge from this dimension.

Deep Pool

36

For many people of faith it is at this level that they find and experience God and this adds a metaphysical perspective to their understanding.

The accompanist not only has this ability to support and understand himself or herself, but this is the level of the space that the accompanist invites the accompanied to explore. A conversation at the higher levels can be helpful, but this sort of knowledge and advice is more easily obtainable. A conversation at a deeper soul level is unusual and is likely to be more profound and meaningful. The accompanying conversation will inevitably inform thinking, feeling and actions, but when understanding is at this deep level there is a more significant impact and a greater opportunity to accept, change and grow.

Jasmine started one of our accompanying conversations by wanting to explore her professional future. Although this was of course important, I sensed that there was something behind this and, rather than enter into this more ordinary conversation, deliberately held my own consciousness at the deeper soul level.

Slowly Jasmine became aware of what was available to her, and I could sense her recognising a deeper problem that she had been wrestling with.

I did not need to do much as she became aware of needing to be loved, being loved and having the permission from herself to be herself. My role as an accompanist was to hold the space while she recognised all of this. I was not finding helpful words and phrases or offering tools of analysis, instead I was in a place where I knew deeply that all was well and the act of accompanying showed her that this place was there for her too.

Accompanying and how it relates to other disciplines

Accompanying is such a part of beautiful human experience that it resonates with people - they have seen it before. How is it different from counselling, spiritual direction, mentoring or even friendship?

When we first explored accompanying in *Accompanying Young People on their Spiritual Quest*, we described what it is not, and in definite detail asserted that it was not befriending or mentoring or counselling. However, with experience we have amended this view - accompanying can be part of all of these practices. Accompanying is an approach, an offer, a state of being which can be brought to each of these different disciplines. The disciplines themselves hold their own ethical parameters to ensure that the practice is responsible and accountable. The meaning of accompanying from the original Latin is 'with bread', the accompaniment being the relish which brings savour and richness to the bread. The disciplines below are the bread, and by adding the extra, richer dimension of the relish of accompanying, the whole process is enhanced and strengthened.

Counselling

A counsellor can accompany their client by stilling themselves and 'working from a deep place within themselves. The contract and the ethical elements of the discipline of counselling are still in place, but the quality and the wisdom of a counsellor who is also an accompanist means that the interchange is at a deeper and more profound level. An accompanist may differ from some counsellors in that they start with the experience and energy of the person accompanied and be led by that rather than by a particular discipline e.g. Gestalt or Jungian.

Mentor

Like accompanying, the mentoring model presupposes that the process is for the benefit of the mentee and that the mentor has wisdom and knowledge to offer. The accompanying mentor will see their role as not providing answers but stimulating their mentee to explore their own situation and equip themselves to find their own direction and approach. Mentors are often sought to help mentees manage roles and tasks so that sometimes the engagement is around specific elements of their role.

A mentor who is also able to access their own stillness and wisdom, as well as their knowledge and experience, enables deeper solutions and ideas to emerge for the mentee.

Befriending

This can be very close to accompanying, as the befriender gives non-critical contact to the person befriended. Also like accompanying, befriending requires a willingness to engage with the befriended with an understanding of the privilege of closeness. The essential difference is that the accompanist is offering this contact by first inhabiting and relating from their own stillness and wisdom. Befriending can take place at an emotional or intellectual level; accompanying brings a deeper, more profound spiritual level to the encounter.

Spiritual Direction

Spiritual directors will ideally work as accompanists, enabling the person under direction to discern the deeper movements of their soul. The best spiritual directors will never impose but will always invite, suggest and in other ways assist the one under direction to find and recognise the unique pattern and rhythm of spirit within the landscape of their personal stories and situations. Our description and illustration of accompanying practice will hopefully encourage best practice in spiritual direction, and perhaps it will also affirm another possibility. Namely, a recognition that the human experience of spirit runs deeper than any religious description or definition, and that it is possible to accompany and to be accompanied across theological and non-theological worldviews. In short, an accompanist does not require a shared theological or philosophical vocabulary as a prerequisite for spiritual conversation nor the witness to the sacred in the story of another.

Understanding the temptations and fears of the ego

Inhabiting this deep space is such a powerful thing to offer, and as I have explored above, being able to readily access this space is a skill which develops with practice. Another skill to help maintain and stay in this space is understanding what can distract you from it and how to manage these distractions.

It is common when starting to meditate to find your mind wandering and to experience a degree of chatter and disruption as you try to find stillness and calm. Similarly during the accompanying session there are a number of ways in which the story of the accompanied person can set hares racing in the mind of the accompanist. If one is aware that this might happen when there is a distraction of one's own experience or history which is ignited through the story of the accompanied, one can gently resist the invitation to explore it and turn it away from one's thoughts.

Paradoxically this can also be helpful, an experience which is brought to the mind of the accompanist may bring a resonance with the experience of the accompanied. There may be an insight attached to this which could be helpful to the accompanied. This means that the skill one needs as an accompanist is not just to resist an invitation to recollect one's own experience, but to dispassionately notice one's own story and check whether it is useful or not. If it is, then gently teasing out the useful element to aid the sacred conversation will be useful. If it is not then gently pushing aside one's own story and refocussing on the accompanied will re-engage the accompanist and enable them to inhabit again that deeper shared level.

Another distraction is the ego of the accompanist. The compassion and empathy which is at the heart of the accompanying conversation can lead the accompanist to try and make the situation right and to rescue the accompanied. Here the ego of the accompanist may want to help and takes it upon itself to try and solve the situation. Although this may work in a mentoring situation, it distracts from a central belief in accompanying – that the accompanied has their own solution and their own understanding and sufficient resources or access to them to make a change. The accompanist must have trust in the process and an unswerving belief that the accompanied person has both the questions and answers within themselves. At another level the accompanist can find themselves checking out how good an accompanist they are and become aware of their own performance. This is a sign that the ego is at work and the focus has shifted from the person accompanied and holding the deep space. An antidote to this distraction is to realign oneself in one's own deeper soul level and return focus, attention and respect to the accompanied.

This does not mean that there should not be times when the accompanist reflects on their own process and assesses whether this has helped, or hindered or could be adjusted and developed in some way. Although the ego is never absent from this process, when this reflection is from a position of curiosity and lightness the demands of the ego do not inhibit the reflective process. Spiritually mature accompanists may be able to embrace the input of the ego with joy and gain some different insights from this. It is a bit like the words of a child in a family gathering – they can sometimes speak truth with a directness and openness which cuts through the verbosity of adulthood. The ego, when understood and not in the driving seat, has potentially a great part to play in speaking these words of truth.

When trust has built up it builds in the accompanist an inner confidence. This is not at all boasting or self-expanding, rather it brings a confidence to the accompanist. This is a sign that the accompanist is competent to hold the space for the accompanied and can be acknowledged as such. In the same way that we feel secure if we leave our car in the garage and the mechanic gives us an assurance that he knows what is wrong and that he can fix it - if we are confident in the process and our own skills and experience the person accompanied can feel safe and relaxed. This enables the person accompanied to be able to enter the accompanying with an experienced and confident guide. These are often uncharted inner territories, so having a good person with knowledge of the soul to guide you is both necessary and enlightening.

The trust and confidence that enables this journey derives in part from the strong conviction the accompanist brings. Namely, the expectation that something of significance will occur. That, if this deep soul space is held carefully and respectfully, whatever needs to be expressed, resolved or explored in the accompanied person will find its voice and speak. A metaphor that works for us is that of a shy echidna hiding in the Australian bush and only venturing out when it feels safe and conditions are right. Stillness, safety and appreciation of the beauty of the inner space are good conditions for the deeper soul messages to emerge.

From time to time the accompanist will need to check that they are inhabiting this deeper zone of the soul or spirit and have not been drawn to a more superficial level. In normal conversations one negotiates the 'level' that feels comfortable. For most of our conversations this will be at a more superficial level and two people will start here and as trust develops the insights and the sharing becomes more profound. Accompanying is different to this as the accompanist makes available a deeper level right from the start of the conversation and continues to offer it as the conversation develops. This can feel strange at first as it challenges some normal 'rules' of conversation, but in our experience many people quickly understand this opportunity and the different possibilities a deep conversation can offer and respond to this offer by using the space without the precursors of checking things out and small talk. For many this experience of being truly seen and deeply respected is profound.

Let me look at you

When I was an external examiner for a university course, I would arrive for my duties to be met by the head of department, Janet. On one occasion Janet said, 'let me look at you'. This was strange at first, but what she was doing changed our meeting, it made me feel like I had really arrived and that I really mattered. This was not a superficial 'being looked at', it was a way of her deeply acknowledging that I had arrived and appreciating me. Consequently our meetings always inhabited a deeper level, one where deep things mattered because both she and I mattered.

This deep respect and knowledge of the other person is at the heart of accompanying.

As the accompanist becomes more practised there are further elements which can emerge. These stories and pictures that come to mind in the accompanist can sometimes seem irrelevant or a distraction. However, these can also be very useful in providing a key for the accompanied to unlock the next part of their story or journey.

This means that the accompanist should have the courage to say the words and share the metaphors that are emerging in your own soul even if they do not feel completely right. Sometimes the slight wrongness of the metaphors enables them to be crafted by the person accompanied so that they become their own. This can be a very uncomfortable place for the ego which wants to make sure that the accompanist is doing a right and proper process, and it also carries the risk of misunderstanding. However, if an insight or metaphor is offered in a loving, respectful way, it is usually okay. For example, 'I'm not sure how helpful this will be to you, but as you are speaking I have a picture in my mind of a bird in a cage' could enable the accompanied to move on, but if it is not useful then it should be put to one side and not pursued by the accompanist.

Offer not tell

The use of metaphor and reflections is such a powerful aspect of accompanying that it needs to be treated carefully. Sometimes as an accompanist you will find that the metaphor or image is so strong that it has an essential and important feel as being supremely important or powerful. Even if you receive something like that it must be offered because, even though you are bringing something from the 'sacred space', you may have got it wrong. Also offering brings about a sense of proper humility and represents the joint journey of curiosity and wonder.

Deep and high – deepness metaphor plus the eternal eyes

The process of accompanying can be seen as both deep and high. The action of deepening the soul and the level of the conversation is central to the endeavour. The normal superficial level of conversation is gently disregarded as the accompanist offers this deeper space to the accompanied. Reflecting on an accompanying session, one person remarked:

49

> The time of accompanying was like opening a treasure chest; I realised that my soul was beautiful, and that there were a multitude of treasures and special gems within that I could look at, rejoice about and use in my life. Deep inside this is the real me.

One of the things the accompanist can do is to invite the accompanied to view themselves and any issue they bring from different perspectives. A question such as: 'What advice would you give yourself if you were speaking to yourself as a friend?' can help to shift a stuck situation or to enable the accompanied to negotiate a block which is stopping the process of understanding. Devices such as this can be useful; however, if the accompanist can help to reframe the situation from a point of deep reflection and wisdom, this can bring more profound and helpful insight and change.

An invitation for the accompanied to view the situation with 'eternal eyes' brings a sense of wisdom and deep goodness into the session. For the accompanied to locate a position of interior wisdom and then reflect on themselves often brings a greater level of self-acceptance and enables a much more eternal frame for problems or situations. This wider and deeper perspective, when one thinks of decades rather than days, weeks or months, can help the accompanied know how transient many 'problems' are.

This offer of an eternal perspective can help someone who is exploring the future, their identity and questions of an open ended and searching nature. Inhabiting this wise place is a great way to ensure that future decisions and directions are rooted in the most important things in life and will honour the soul of that person. This will not only support the individual positively but has a potential impact on those that are around them.

The Art and Practice of Accompanying

The act of accompanying thus requires practice and reflection. It requires concentration, balance and an inner peace to build a positive and joyful place for the accompanied person to explore.

It is an art in that it requires great sensitivity and creativity. It also requires an integration of mind, body and soul. The 'studio' for the accompanist is a respectful place where there is expectation that something good will happen. The art of the accompanist develops as they offer this space to others – where the accompanist sees folk arriving with their own stories and worlds and leaving with deeper knowledge and understanding. The art of accompanying is subtle and beautiful and is truly a great gift.

Phil's comment:

Maxine's own unique soul work shines in this chapter. Her discussion about the role and place of ego is of the highest quality. In this, and also in relation to what she says about the offering or withholding of metaphors and associated stories, she highlights a fluid capacity for inner dialogue and immediate evaluative choices. Trust and confidence are central themes in this discussion. The accompanist is the one who trusts in their capacities and who trusts in the rightness and goodness of the process 'that something of significance will occur'. In this way we see that the capacities of an accompanist are slow grown rather than acquired. We also are presented with a vision of a wonderfully peaceful practice that avoids the tortuous phenomenon of professional self-consciousness. Can you feel the invitation and the aspiration calling to that deeper part of yourself, and do you sense the kindness and warmth behind the door that is being held open for you?

In my next chapter we will explore a practical context in which such soul work is expressed in an organisational setting.

ACCOMPANYING GROUPS AND ORGANISATIONS

Accompanying is a practice of making a deliberate space for conversations of the soul. The idea of this space is to ground the person in the essence and spirit of their being. In the wisdom narratives of most religions, and in the field of spirituality studies, this kind of grounding not only locates the individual in a life that emerges from the centre, but also places them in relationship to a larger mystery, sense of place and belonging in the world. This placement and location is an essential alignment. From this alignment the true life of the person unfolds in meaning, joy, happiness and service. The soul aligned life is a restorative and healing presence in the world. It is an abundant life; a helpful and hopeful life. A life that contributes to making the world a kinder and safer space.

This kind of space, conversation and location is also necessary and desired for groups and organisations. A group that makes space for the sacred and for the care of the soul will become a group that is connected and integrated at deep levels of wisdom, respect, kindness and creativity. Such elements of group life cannot be mandated and enforced but may be nurtured through the practice of accompanying at a group level. Making time and space for the accompanying conversation in the life of the group provides an intense experience of interconnectedness through the fusion of soul connection. This fusion is powerfully transformative for individuals within the group and also for the nature of the group relationship in its corporate function. As I write these words, the vision of Thomas Merton comes to mind:

> At the centre of our being is a point of
> nothingness which is untouched by sin and by

illusion, a point of pure truth, a point or spark which belongs entirely to God, which is never at our disposal, from which God disposes of our lives, which is inaccessible to the fantasies of our own mind or the brutalities of our own will. This little point of nothingness and of absolute poverty is the pure glory of God in us ... It is like a pure diamond, blazing with the invisible light of heaven. It is in everybody, and if we could see it we would see these billions of points of light coming together in the face and blaze of a sun that would make all the darkness and cruelty of life vanish completely ... I have no program for this seeing. It is only given. But the gate of heaven is everywhere (1989).

We invite you to consider Merton's vision above in relation to a group that is part of your workplace or community. If the 'pure diamond blazing with the invisible light of heaven' that resides in each member of your group were to become seen, known, acknowledged and welcomed, what would that look like? Can you imagine this hidden combustible energy as a permeating presence and force in your group life? The very same conditions and principles that allow space for an individual to become present to this deeper and essential part of their humanity may also be applied to the group setting. It is the mission of the accompanist to assist the workplace, or community group, to see each other, and the group as a whole, in a new way. Together the goal is to discover the essential ground of their corporate being as sacred. Metaphorically speaking, the vision of their workplace as a common shrub is transformed into one of a burning bush that cannot be consumed.

> Earth's crammed with heaven,
> And every common bush afire with God;
> But only he who sees, takes off his shoes;
> The rest sit round it and pluck blackberries.
> (Elizabeth Barrett Browning, 1806-1861)

At this point I want to talk about my own story about workplace accompanying. Many years ago I read about the practice of a certain leader in a faith-based organisation who spoke of creating a generous space in his staff meetings for soul talk. His view was that if the team prioritised a space for centring and renewal as the first priority of business, the remainder of the agenda would flow in a more efficient and fruitful way. To some extent this is a faith-based proposition in itself. I was attracted by the logic of this suggestion and decided to adapt it to my own setting.

I work in a busy and resource challenged, not-for-profit, faith-based tertiary education institute (Tabor). I manage a diverse faculty and suite of programs and, as part of this management, meet monthly with faculty leaders in my team for corporate discussion, decision making and regulatory procedures. It is not as dull as it sounds, but our meeting agendas are full and we do function in a culture of complex workloads and relentless deadlines. The temptation is to be in a hurry, to cut out anything and everything not obviously and directly related to getting the work done. Does this sound familiar?

I noticed in our organisational meeting agenda template a standard dot-point space for an opening prayer. As an act of faith and resistance, I decided to leverage this dot-point into a 40-minute space for the team to engage at a level of conversation that has to do with the soul of their journey and workspace. The space that I facilitate is invitational, unhurried, resourced by a short reading, activity and/or question/s that scaffold participation. Silent pauses in the ebb and flow of this unhurried, reflective conversation are normalised. This part of the meeting is contemplative dialogue rather than business discussion. I have initiated and led this space with the intention to draw my staff into the process rather than impose it.

My observation has been that this space, in which we drop down beneath our role titles and portfolios and engage each other at a deeper and more human level, has proved fruitful and immensely enjoyable. Unsolicited, appreciative feedback from the team members has been consistent. As the manager of the team I cannot be completely sure of the way in which the power dynamics of my relationship with them influence the nature of this feedback, but my impression is that we are onto something beneficial and fruitful. A couple of years ago I invited some of the long-serving members of my team to comment on their experience of these times. In eliciting their commentary, I used what is referred to as a phenomenological method of interviewing, editing and interpreting their stories. The edited versions of the stories and my interpretations of them unfold below; the names of the storytellers have been changed. I believe this material illustrates examples of what can happen when accompanying conversations are given space and structure within a workplace setting.

Michelle:

I recall in the midst of a fairly big time of turmoil for me, we had a meeting and going to that I was feeling vulnerable and thinking I just need to be really careful that I [don't] show [my] emotions. I don't actually recall the text that you even read but I know it was [from] the psalms and talking about being still, which is what you teach us in the way that you present the beginning of the meeting where we have that time of really listening and thinking about what it is for us that day. I guess the thing that hit me was just to be still. That was so transforming for me because I hadn't at that point given myself permission to stop. I just thought I had to keep going to deal with what was going on in my life, so it actually was a turning point in me. [L]earning that it's okay just to stop and the world will still go on whether I stop or run around in circles. It's just simple, but that was something that touched me significantly.

It meant that I was no longer jumping between my own chaotic mind and the meeting and trying to stay in tune like I had probably learnt to do. I was more focussed on the meeting, I know that for a fact. And when I felt my mind racing again, I just thought *just be*

61

still 'and know that I am God', just that stillness. And I find that every meeting I feel like that. Having that space beforehand is that time where I actually know that I'm 'gonna stop. And then I can just focus on the next thing.

I think people value it immensely. Some may find it uncomfortable if they haven't been used to it because I certainly found it uncomfortable in the beginning because I wasn't used to that type of environment in a workplace. When I heard that we would do this in our meetings, at first it reminded me of church too much. But when [I experienced it] I was like, *Oh that's different it's not church, it's not.* [This practice] has really influenced my own spirituality. I feel calmer because of it and I feel hope that the evidence of that will come out in the future. I talk to people and respond to things and I feel like that is happening even now. At times before I would have been more reactive and I am calmer because I practice that space now.

Commentary:

Michelle tells a story of a conversion experience that she describes as a 'turning point'. Her choice of language is interesting. She says that this is a turning point in her rather than the more external for her. What has turned? Her experience of being in the world. She recognises in a new way that her influence in the world is small, limited and, in a way, non-essential. This awareness is experienced as calming, hopeful and re-connecting. The connection is back to herself as an integrated person, who is no longer, 'jumping between' states of consciousness. The connection is also to the work of the meeting in which she is part, and to her general way of relating to herself and others. She describes her conversion as 'a fact' and her new sense of emotional presence and outlook as 'evidence' that something important has changed in her. The locus for change is her participation in a guided contemplative practice that has involved engagement with texts and with conversation. Interestingly she cannot recall details of the texts but clearly describes both the impact of the exercise and the style of the facilitator. This practice has become an important space for her that she carries over into other spaces in her life. She notes the tension and paradox of a spiritual practice that is 'not church' and its unusual placement within the workplace. In her story, Michelle mentions the word 'God', which highlights the transcendental nature of her new awareness: she is not perpetually, personally responsible to control and manage all the events and aspects relating to her worlds of concern. Somehow, she senses it is 'okay to stop', periodically, and it is this act of stopping that transforms the nature and qualities of her doing.

Mike:

[W]e went [off site] for a planning meeting and we [started with] that space and you read a piece from *The Unlikely Pilgrimage of Harold Fry*,[1] and [the narrative was about] set[ting] out to the mailbox, [to] post a letter, but then [to] see where it takes us, where it goes. We c[a]me with an agenda of what we hope[d] to achieve that day, but there was something liberating about that moment. What was amazing was that it facilitat[ed] creativity. I think the action [of reading and reflection] itself made [us] relax [into] the day. That induces and informs creativity. So at the end of the day it was a good meeting and [afterwards] I actually went out and got the book. And I read it.

---

1 A novel by Rachel Joyce, 2013.

[Our practice] creates that space where you can pay attention and [notice] the [seemingly] trivial things that we don't [normally] see as significant. [T]he capacity to notice makes it worthwhile. And it's special. [I]t allowed me to notice being with my colleagues, being with what was said on the day; it gave me the opportunity to be conscious.

[W]hen you come into a meeting [where] you get straight on to the agenda, [people] tend to latch on to [their] own agendas, [their] own expectations, whereas with this contemplative practice, it allows the opportunity for that to be suspended, and it's not necessarily a conscious thing. It's just the consequence, the benefit, that brings us to that place of dropping those defences, dropping that need to plough through and get things done, the need to hold onto something. It just frees us. It takes us out of that rut and wakes us up to possibilities, to new possibilities.

The ironic thing is that we could say we are [too] busy [for this space], but for me the thing that I value is it enhances productivity. [T]his [space] is my connection with God, this is my church time. [C]oming from a really legalistic church background, it's something that I just look forward to. It's a connection, a possibility of discovering something new. [It] gives us the opportunity for creativity, for flow.

Commentary:

Mike tells us a story about his experience of a planning day that turned out to be different to his initial expectations. A small, contemplative practice not only begins the day, its essence infuses the day and the nature of what happens throughout. Mike tells us that the practice enables him to loosen his grip on the agenda and to become present to the people in the room and to the possibilities of difference. He relaxes, he lets go, he embraces the opportunity. He sees things he might otherwise have missed. He experiences energy, creativity and productivity in the process. His story is one of irony, reconciliation and completion. In-between the lines of the agenda he re-discovers the meaning of faith community in a way that also enhances the professional outcome of the meeting. There is a sense of closing the circle, of encountering an abundance of life in which the worlds of the professional and personal become more fully integrated to the mutual enhancement of both.

Rebecca:

[A]round Easter last year in one of our faculty meetings, there was an article that was read about something, I cannot remember the title of the article. It was a notion of, 'Do prayers hold planes up, or do prayers make planes fly?', or something like that. I think it was about the relationship between intention and prayer and how God works in that space anyway. And there was an invitation after that to draw what we heard or what resonated with us in that space. It was such a beautiful and fruitful discussion that happened within the staff members and I really enjoyed the difference. [Y]ou learn so much about your colleagues when you're all in that space. [Although] you've heard the same thing, [there are] different interpretations. It was really, really beautiful. Especially [because of] the subject of faith, because you assume that people have similar outlooks [to] you, because that's your outlook. [T]hen you hear something and you're like, 'Oh wow! That's where you're coming from.' It really stuck with me, that experience, so I ended up taking that same article and I read it to some of my students in the class. And it was a profound moment for them too because we kind of opened the space up to listen, to reflect, to draw – which again is odd because it's a childlike activity. And [we] share[d] with each other our experiences of that. [This story is]one of many [from our faculty times]. It doesn't fail to give opportunity for creativity and adjoining; you get to know your colleagues more. You have the benefit of your own reflection, but I love the shared experience as well. That's the joy of doing it in a meeting space. [Though it] is odd to think about a contemplative space in a meeting.

Commentary:

Rebecca relates an experience of being surprised and empowered by joy. She listens to the reading of an article, the title of which she cannot remember and the content of which she has a sense, but few details. However, it is this sense of the article, rather than its structural and conceptual details, which is integral to her experience. A significant part of this sense relates to the paradox of the article's subject (faith) and invitation to self-reflect through the medium of a children's activity (drawing), in the context of a business meeting. The unusual juxtaposition of these factors evokes both a feeling of oddness and an unfolding vision of something 'really, really beautiful'. The oddness of the experience as something socially unorthodox seems to intensify the joy. Perhaps in part this can be traced to Rebecca's position and passion as an academic sociologist. The movement from her assumption of collective faith as one common view to a heightened awareness of diversity and its value indicates this.

The joy that Rebecca experiences is seen to stay with her beyond the meeting and then overflows and re-creates itself in the transformation of the classroom space. This indicates a spiritual phenomenon. The joy has made a home within her, it creates a new space. This new space is then seen to shape the space of her classroom in which the joy finds its re-formation in the permeation of her practice.

Closing considerations:

The stories and commentaries that form the central part of this chapter illustrate the potential for accompanying practices in workplace and community settings. The idea behind this illustration is that conversations of the soul have their place in public life and in fact are essential to the productivity and fruitfulness of working organisations and groups. In addition, accompanying conversation humanises the experience of work, thus it functions as an ethical and just practice that is valid and important for its own sake.

We imagine that there will be as many ways to enable and facilitate accompanying practices within workplace and community settings as there are contexts and willing, imaginative leaders and managers. Our encouragement to leaders and managers such as this is to have a go and take the risk of exploration, experimentation and implementation.

As I close this chapter I would like to leave you with a comment from therapist and author Thomas Moore. His insight in speaking of the place of soul in work and public life suggests a spiritual resolution to the contemporary dilemma of work-life balance and its associated performance stress:

> One perhaps surprising source of potential soul in our work is failure. The dark cloud of failure that shadows our earnest efforts is to some extent an antidote for overly high expectations. Our ambition for success and perfection in work drives us on, while worries

about failure keep us tied to the soul in work. When ideas of perfection dive downward into the lower regions of the soul, out of that gesture of incarnation comes human achievement. We may feel crushed by failure, but our lofty aims may need some spoiling if they are to play a creative role in human life. Perfection belongs to an imaginary world. According to traditional teaching, it is the life-embedded soul, not soaring spirit that defies humanity...

Failure is a mystery, not a problem.

... By appreciating failure with imagination, we reconnect it with success. Without the connection, work falls into grand narcissistic fantasies of success and dismal feelings of failure. But as a mystery, failure is not mine; it is an element in the work I am doing. (Moore, 1992, pp. 196-197)

In this brief commentary above we are presented with an insight that has the potential to transform both the life experience of individuals in the workplace as well as the quality and nature of accomplishment by an organisation.

It is insights such as these and the conversations they potentially evoke that will allow an organisation and the working teams within it to cultivate a rich economy of spirit - should there exist the willingness to engage.

Maxine's comment:

Phil illustrates in this chapter how the practice of accompanying can be extended and be allowed to infuse the busiest of organisations. 'This is so urgent – we'll have to slow down' is a counterintuitive message in our busy and frenetic world. Phil has shown that when one has the courage to honour the spiritual life of the person and organisation the experience releases folk and systems so that they are more real, human and efficient. By unpicking and reflecting on the words of participants, truths are revealed and uncover the powerful dynamics of meaning when accompanying and being accompanied by others.

In the next chapter I reflect on how these can help bring healing and restoration.

Accompanying in Transitions, Healing & Reconciliation

When we first explored accompanying it was focussed on young people. We could see that moving from childhood to becoming an adult was a tricky transitional phase - it was not just the pressure of changing hormones or facing the newness of increased responsibility for oneself, it was coming to terms with a deep change in identity - the possibility of future paths unfolding, and a recognition of living through a profound time.

At times of transition there are different processes going on. As well as looking forward, there is a need for the past to be okay for there to be no difficult unresolved issues. A journey is so much easier when we leave a settled and resolved situation behind. For young people there are childhood fears, concerns and celebrations which need to be acknowledged and embraced to give a solid foundation on which to build their future adult identities. Accompanying a young person during this time may involve giving them space to reconcile difficulties in the past and encouraging and helping them to heal rifts or pain that is behind them. It also involves being alongside them as they open the future ahead of them and gather the courage to imagine and try different ways of being themselves on the way to discovering their own authentic nature and truth.

From time to time in our lives there are watershed moments that require reflection and discernment if we are to make good choices. It is at these times a deep, sound accompanist can offer a gift of space and safety to fully explore options and possibilities. Reconciliation, both internal and with others, and healing can be part of this process as well as exploring future possibilities.

As our work is with young people this has been our focus, but recently personal experience has taken my own role as an accompanist into new realms – accompanying my grandson and accompanying someone as he died.

Accompanying a toddler

When I first heard that I was going to be a grandmother, friends and acquaintances rejoiced with me and told me how this was a very special relationship which was different to the mother/child bond. I had the privilege of being there when Theo was born, as he took his first breath, and there is a photo of me rapt in wonder as I looked on this little soul at the start of his life.

There are many jobs to do as a grandmother, but I have found the most important of these is to accompany Theo. To be with him in the moment, calming my own agenda and aims and simply being alongside him. Wandering around a garden and becoming aware of stones which need to be placed on a brick wall, stroking the dog with enough time and focus for it to be a real and important event, eating a strawberry which has been green for weeks and is finally ready so we can 'eat it'.

Parents are busy people and of course are able to share moments like these, but as a grandmother I can stretch out these moments and make a larger space for them.

Curiously, I find that it is me that is accompanied for a lot of the time we are together, it is me who is being taught by Theo how to relax in the moment, how to enjoy and delight in the curious nature of the world, how to be open to things around me without prejudice or prejudgement.

This halcyon picture is part of a toddler's experience but so are the 'terrible twos' and the internal distress a toddler feels when he is overwhelmed by frustration and disappointment. Times when his young ego is thwarted and the betrayal and injustice are almost too much to bear. Accompanying has a role here too. I try to centre my soul in the deep safe space where all is calm and quiet and all is well, to bring a soft certainty to the desperate situation and stillness in the frenetic thrashing. Keeping calm when someone is hitting you and saying that they don't like you is really difficult and, as I say to friends, something that one rarely tolerates when it is an adult doing it, but locating a pool of compassion and offering it is a beautiful thing to do.

The lovely thing about accompanying Theo has been a growth in my understanding and wisdom. I recognise that there is often a distressed toddler in grownups that I know and in myself. Recognising this, I want to give myself permission to be in the moment and be open to a sense of wonder and engagement with the world. It has been a wonderful experience for which I am deeply thankful.

Accompanying someone as they are dying

If our teenage years are spring, then the time of our death is autumn, as the possibilities of growth which are promised in the spring are quietly closed down as our lives draw to a close. Accompanying someone as they pass through this transition can be a similar gift and can be helpful and profound. There are seminal moments in our lives as human beings and the closing moments of a life are one of them. The final words on the death bed, which are often quite shallow, are recorded and passed on as important. The curiosity of death, with no certainty of knowing what comes next, imbues a different quality to a relationship at the end of life when a person slips away to another realm where they can no longer be reached.

Observing the passing away of someone is a foreshadow of one's own death and passing; all the while one knows that, at some stage in the future, this will be you. There is no escaping this final call, and being with someone when they are on this last journey is a strong reminder of the fact of our future journey.

Unlike other episodes in our lives, dying is one which cannot be treated lightly. It commands a deeper contact, a deeper knowing, an engagement not just with the stuff of dying but of the meaning of dying. This is not just in the last moments of life, as the last breaths are taken and the soul prepares to go, it is also apparent as the person achieves an understanding of their own mortality and recognises that their life will soon be over.

It is in this context that I accompanied my uncle for the last few months of his life. It started with a superficial arrangement, a simple letter saying that on his visits to the hospital he had become aware that all the patients were there in pairs – a Noah's Ark arrangement as two by two people filed into the consultancy room to hear the latest prognosis and receive the next round of treatment. He had become aware that he was alone, a single soul, shuffling around with no 'other' person to be with him. My uncle and I go back a long way, 'uncle' being a title given to a friend of the family rather than an indication of a filial relationship; he was my Godfather. As an atheist the promise he made at my Christening was to look out for me, rather than to bring me up in the faith. And the simple letter asked if I could be there with him, for him – of course I said yes. During those final nine months I continued to be alongside him whilst his healthy, strong body was slowly diminished and weakened by a blood disease and failing organs.

The initial agreement to go with him was at a functional level; I drove and waited with him in the lonely place with lots of chairs filled with others waiting for their call to spend time with the consultant, being with him while the doctor, the nurses and the blood takers went through their routines and services to try and make him well. Slowly, I started to understand that the functional level of being there, although it was useful, was not why I was there. It was not even just for emotional support; there was something else that was there as a possibility, an opportunity to be within the situation with a deeper sense of meaning – to truly accompany my uncle as he was going through a very difficult time.

There is so much stuff and busyness that surrounds a difficult diagnosis. Letters for appointments at the hospital seemed to come through almost every day, and the visits to health professionals and by health professionals were like a cloud of distraction to deflect the mind from the real understanding of what was going on and the knowledge that this was the beginning of the end. Besides, my uncle really didn't want to know this, did not want any discussion about death or dying. He accepted the invitation to become lost in medical processes with an underlying belief that medicine cures and all would be well.

Aside from the hectic medical roundabout there were many hours at the bedside. At the end he had diminished to half his normal weight and lay almost motionless in a bed with others servicing every bodily need. From time to time he was sad, from time to time he was cross and critical, a strong man whose body had deserted him and left him with something that he didn't recognise or know. Accompanying often meant just being there, no words, not even explicit gestures, but sitting next to the bed and strongly residing in the deep positive part of myself. This enabled me to accept the diminishment of my uncle's body whilst accepting his strong soul and personhood.

Although we didn't talk about it, my acceptance of this, I think, brought some sort of reconciliation and healing. At a deep level in the shared silence we both were aware of something whilst not being positive, having a sense of inevitable deep okay-ness.

It is very hard to know if my accompanying benefited my uncle, and if it did benefit him, in what way did it do this? I do know that my own soul was deeply touched by this closeness and the intimacy of being with him through these months and as he died brought so much learning and soul growth for me. What a privilege it is to be with someone when the stuff of the world falls away from them and they have an understanding of the nakedness of their own soul, and even if he didn't, I did. My own mortality was standing alongside his and the impact on me was huge.

This accompanying needed a lot of personal courage from me. I now understand why carers adopt the caring busyness role that they do, as it keeps the more powerful realisation of the very terminal nature of death away. I learnt to inhabit the very deepest parts of my soul where there is stability, safety and peace. While I was there I sat next to him holding this quiet peace that was necessary for me and hopefully helpful for him.

What this has taught me

More than anything accompanying my uncle has taught me how to centre myself at the very deepest level when things are tough. I have gained a real understanding of the power of calm presence where as an accompanist I occupied a safe, stable peaceful place and was then able to open to the fear, hurt and worry in the other person whilst offering them assurance that I was firmly based and secure.

It has taught me that holding this space is not an ego thing, it is enabled by opening to grace and trust. It is not a superficial learning, it is knowledge from having been in that place many times whilst there is turmoil above, and knowing that at the heart of everything there is safety and love.

The people that have accompanied me have been able to hold any issue, any fear or worry I have brought into that calm space of security and peace. Although it doesn't make the difficult stuff go away, it brings a deeper perspective and meaning into the situation with an assurance that my soul is well.

Phil's comment:

In this chapter, my attention is drawn to what Maxine says about the importance of resolving the past. I notice often the restlessness that so many people experience as a symptom of something that has not been processed or framed. I think we have to *have* our experiences and not simply endure them or move on from them. At some level we need to make sense of what has gone before and extract from each and every event of our lives something restorative and redemptive. This is possible, it can be done, and there is a pathway to these resolutions. The accompanist and the philosophy of accompanying speak to us of the essential need to make the space and time for a way of being with the past that allows the resolution to appear. It will come as a gift, a wisdom from our deepest interior and also from the connection between our sacred essence and the universal consciousness (God) in which we all 'live and move and have our being' (Acts 17:28, NIV).

Maxine tells us about an experience of accompanying and being accompanied by a toddler, her grandson. This is a mutual experience. At times Maxine learns from Theo. At other times Maxine is called to practice stillness in the face of Theo's chaos as he has yet to cultivate this deeper inner path for himself. This practice is not only one of support but also of silent education. As Maxine relates to her grandson from a still centre, her way of being *with* him will evoke the cultivation of depth *from* him. Her soul presence is nutrient to the seeds of his. Theo's presence speaks to Maxine of the child within herself and others in its mixture of beauty and insecurity. This awareness evokes empathy in her approach to some of the difficult adults she encounters. Perhaps also an empathy towards herself.

Maxine's story of being with her uncle through the process of dying is deeply touching and insightful. What speaks to me is the experience of engaging one's own mortality through proximity to the dying of another. The posture of leaning into our mortality rather than denying it, I find deeply attractive and restorative. Maxine wonders if her uncle has benefited from her accompanying silence yet is not dependent on an answer in the affirmative to validate her offering. As an accompanist she offers her presence as a gift sufficient in itself and trusts simply in the rightness and goodness of the act. Here again we see a liberating perspective on vocation that is free from an obsession with self-evaluation and striving. This expression stands as an invitation to each of us to find a way of simple being and offering in line with our own gifts and opportunities.

This chapter with its deeply personal and narrative quality provides a worthy and fitting conclusion to our conversation. If you have made it this far with us we congratulate you on the completion of a worthy discipline. In my final short chapter I hold out an invitation for you to consider your active, ongoing response to the notion of accompanying.

AN INVITATION TO OFFER YOURSELF AS AN ACCOMPANIST

In this book we have defined, illustrated and explained what we mean by the art of accompanying. The ultimate purpose of the book is to entice you, the reader, to jump on board with the practice and to lend a hand. It is our firm belief that people all around us are in desperate need of soul care. This has always been the case and likely always will be. In Australia, my country, and the land of my heart, our spirituality has been described as 'a shy hope in the heart, a whisper in the mind' (Bouma, 2006, p.

2). This phrase implies the existence of a fragile spiritual instinct that left unattended remains unnamed, unarticulated and therefore barely accessible. The outcome is that everyday people are left without vocabulary, ritual and practices that enable access to the inner life and the resources of the soul. In particular, people are left without meaningful connection to historical wisdom narratives and communities of practice. I do not believe this dangerous existential gap can be adequately bridged by resilience workshops or mindfulness techniques that have detached from the philosophical and religious bodies which give them definition, substance and meaning. Such have their place and offer forms of assistance in coping but do not replace the crucial need for the sustained inner journey and developing relationship to the soul. As David Tacey puts it:

> The collapse of religion in the lives of modern people has caused an inner upheaval that is rarely acknowledged by the secular world. Secularism likes to imagine that we can get along quite nicely without this ancient system of 'superstition', as it calls it, and it ignores the catastrophe that such a loss has entailed for

the soul. Religion played a more important role in our lives than many imagine, and without this guidance we are in a state of disorientation (2016, p26).

The renowned 20th Century theologian, Karl Rahner argued that Christianity in the future would have a mystical rather than institutional or social/cultural basis. His observation was that the social support and motivation for participation in the Christian faith had collapsed in western societies and that therefore each person would need to discover a different, deeply personal motivation for faith. He encouraged the church to rediscover methods and mediums through which individuals could receive the help they needed to undertake the mystical journey. His belief was that a form of Ignatian spirituality[2] would help, in association with personal guides and small groups. This in fact has come to pass to an extent as is evidenced by the many contemporary resources and opportunities available for

---

2 Ignatian spirituality is a tradition that follows the form and teaching of St. Ignatius Loyolla (1491-1556), the founding father of the Jesuits (Society of Jesus). Ignatian spirituality has experienced a renaissance in its expression and popularity during the last 50 years.

everyday people to explore the personal meaning of the Ignatian tradition for their own lives.[3] The intention of this book is not to argue for a particular tradition of spiritual practice but for the need of spiritually formed people willing to assist others to find the path that best fits and makes sense in their context. Everyone can access the soul and take the inner journey but not without the skilled help of an experienced guide.

The nature of our contemporary social context in developed societies is multicultural, pluralistic and secular. Thus an accompanist will need to be one who has grounded themselves through a particular tradition but who is able from such a position to assist the accompanied in finding the form and style appropriate to their own story. This approach is beautifully expressed in a description by Pico Iyer of the relationship between the Dalai Lama and the Trappist monk and author, Thomas Merton:

> The last time I saw His Holiness, he told me how, growing up in isolated Lhasa, he thought that Buddhism was the greatest religion on

---

3 See for example the Loyola Press public website: https://www.ignatianspirituality.com/

earth. He'd barely seen another. Then, relatively soon after going into exile, he was visited by a Christian brother from Kentucky and saw that this man's devotion, clarity, commitment to reality and potential was no less great, and that Catholicism had its own singular beauty and strength. For many, this course would be a more fitting one than Buddhism (2017, pp. 137-138).

Those who know of Merton's own spiritual journey will appreciate the mutual accompanying effect of the meeting of these two spiritual men. Each was able to recognise within the other a commonality of space, depth and enchantment. The engagement across tradition, from a position of depth within a tradition, is the way of the accompanist.

The desperate need of the hour is for women and men who have travelled an inner path to make themselves available to exegete the barely noticeable, subterranean tremors of the inarticulate spirituality of others. Not to impose a tradition or structure but to assist the fragile, yet resonant spiritual longing to explore language, forms and practices that fit the unique shape of the emergent soul. A colleague of mine has crafted a poignant phrase:

'The story not told is not known' (Macaitis, 2017). What she means by this is that the practice of telling the stories of our deeper values, sense of self and life brings to consciousness the spiritual aspect of our being. Who will stand in this kind of existential gap? Who will take the time and care necessary to enable the dumb to speak? Who will hold the space long enough, bearing with the discomfort of resisting the easy answer, of filling the void with words, doctrines and pre-constructed answers? Who will introduce the uninitiated to their own depths? Who will bear with their own 'clunkiness' as a practitioner long enough to develop the unique skills of deep spiritual listening and questioning? Who is willing to forgo the role of the therapeutic problem solver and to act instead as midwife for the messy business of birthing the soul? Who is willing to let go, to trust the space, to believe in the rightness of the process?

Our hope, dear reader, is that such a person just might be you.

References

Bouma, G. (2006). *Australian Soul: religion and spirituality in the Twenty-first Century*. Port Melbourne, Victoria: Cambridge University Press

Green, M. & Christian, C. (1998). *Accompanying young people on their spiritual quest*. London: Church House Publishing.

Iyer, P. (2017). Thomas Merton and the realization of us. In J. M. Sweeney (Ed.), *What I am living for: Lessons from the life and writings of Thomas Merton* (pp. 137-138): Notre Dame, IN: Ave Maria Press.

Leunig, M. (2004). *When I talk to you: A cartoonist talks to God*. Pymble, NSW: HarperCollins.

Merton, T. (1989). *Conjectures of a guilty bystander*. New York: Doubleday.

Moore, T. (1992). *Care of the soul: A guide for cultivating depth and sacredness in everyday life*. New York: HarperCollins.

Rahner, K. (1999). *Encounters with silence*. South Bend, IN: St. Augustine's Press.

Tacey, D. (2016). Spiritual education: drawing out what is within. In Daughtry, P. & Devenish, S. (Eds.). (2016). *Spirituality for youth work: New vocabulary, concepts and practices* (pp. 16-31). Newcastle upon Tyne: Cambridge Scholars Publishing.

INFLUENCES:

Aristotle, (1998). *Nicomachean ethics*. New York: Dover
　　　Publications.

De Waal, E. (2011). *A retreat with Thomas Merton: A seven-day
　　　spiritual journey* (3rd ed.). London: Canterbury
　　　Press.

Eliot, T. S. (1969). *The complete poems and plays*. London:
　　　Faber and Faber.

Furlong, M. (1971). *Travelling in*. Boston: Cowley
　　　Publications.

May, G. G. (2005). *The dark night of the soul: A psychiatrist
　　　explores the connection between darkness and spiritual
　　　growth* (1st HarperCollins pbk. ed.). San Francisco:
　　　HarperSanFrancisco.

Merton, T. (1972). *New seeds of contemplation*. New York: New
　　　Directions Books.

Merton, T. (1987). *Spiritual direction and meditation*.
　　　Collegeville, Minnesota: The Liturgical Press.

Palmer, P. J. (2000). *Let your life speak: listening for the voice of
　　　vocation*. San Francisco: Jossey-Bass, A Wiley
　　　Imprint.

Palmer, P. J., Tucker, E., Jackson, M., Center for, C., & Renewal. (2007). *The courage to teach: Exploring the inner landscape of a teacher's life* (10th anniversary ed.). San Francisco, California: Jossey-Bass, A Wiley Imprint.

Rahner, K. (1958). *Happiness through prayer.* London: Clonmore & Reynolds.

Rahner, K. (1979). *Ignatius of Loyola:* Collins.

Rolf, V. M. (2018). *An explorer's guide to Julian of Norwich.* Downers Grove, IL: IVP Academic, an imprint of InterVarsity Press.

Shah, I. (1974). *Thinkers of the East.* Great Britain: Penguin.

Tacey, D. J. (2000). *Re-enchantment: The new Australian spirituality.* Sydney, NSW, Australia: HarperCollins Publishers.

Tacey, D. J. (2003). *The spirituality revolution: the emergence of contemporary spirituality.* Pymble, NSW: HarperCollins.

Tacey, D. J. (2013). *Gods and diseases: Making sense of our physical and mental wellbeing* (1st ed.). Hove, East Sussex New York: Routledge.

Vaughan-Lee, L. (1995). *Travelling the path of love: Sayings of Sufi Masters. California: The Golden Sufi Centre.* California: The Golden Sufi Centre.

Phil Daughtry:

Is best described as an intellectual and contemplative with a love for silence, meditative writing, the Australian bush, red wine and family. He works as Dean of Faculty (Humanities and Social Sciences) and Dean of Students for Tabor College in Adelaide and Perth.

Maxine Green:

Has a life-long interest in youth work, social anthropology and spirituality. She lives with her family on a smallholding in Suffolk, England. Her previous roles include National Advisor for Youth Work for the Church of England and Principal of YMCA George Williams College.